P9-DYP-221

Michel Devillers

Chartres Cathedral

SECALIB

From Carnutes forest to Péguy's pilgrimages

Do we know Chartres? It is the common and unhappy fate of the great symbols of our civilisation that they are not fully understood. In our subconscious there is a mental image of things in our culture which we are aware of only in the broadest sense. They range from Péguy's pilgrimages to the adventures of Asterix in Carnutes forest. As soon as the time comes to ascertain precisely how far our knowledge goes it would appear that we are frequently embarrassed. In this guide book we would like to present all the facts in as succinct a manner as possible. We shall avoid to the best of our ability being too simplistic or too pedantic, but we hope to leave you with a somewhat more lasting impression than is normally the case with those who visit Chartres for the first and sometimes the last time: a cathedral disappearing over the horizon through the train window.

Enough said. This guide book is essentially dedicated to facilitating an understanding of the cathedral, despite the fact that Chartres isn't merely the cathedral (for who has heard of Saint Aignan's church or the remarkable Cellier de Loëns?). But first of all a few pages of historical background. A cathedral, afther all, is not a meteorite, and it is extremely important to establish the origin, or more exactly the origins of this extraordinary building.

A little history...
From the water of Autrium well to the cult of the Virgin

It is very interesting to observe that chance hardly ever exists in Art. Certain places seem to be predestined in some way. "There are places where the spirit breathes", wrote Maurice Barrès, and even if over the course of the centuries profound religious, cultural etc. upheavals intervene, the spiritual roots live on. The new ideas, far from leading to a withering scepticism, in fact reinforce the original ideas: like attracts like. This is certainly the case in Chartres. The tourist in a hurry must be astonished to find rising up in the middle of the plains of Beauce this enormous building which seems to bring heaven and earth together. In fact, Chartres is one of the most ancient shrines in the whole of France. Caesar mentions its existence under the name of **Autricum** (etymology: Autra ie Eure) and mentions the Druid ceremonies in Carnutes forest. A mysterious water cult was celebrated there (we must remember the essential rôle played by the elements in pagan religions), in a temple situated next to a well whose water had numerous curative powers. The miraculous qualities of this sanctuary, therefore, must also be emphasised. Around this cult grew a relatively large Gallo-Roman town which came to boast an amphitheatre and numerous roads leading from it thus allowing its influence to permeate the whole region. Thus the town's economic importance soon became as great

Atlantes on the Royal Portal.

(Over the page)

The Rod of Jesse (to right of west front, seen from inside).

as its religious importance, for its situation at the centre of a crossroads ensured its rapid expansion and development. But this also made it a tempting prey for all eventual invaders.

From Barbarian invasions to the building of the cathedral : the miracles of faith

The town was almost completely destroyed after being laid to ruin by Barbarian invasions. The inhabitants had to escape to the plateau and construct ramparts. In the IVth century the first episcopal church was founded, and in the IXth century the future fame of Chartres was assured by an endowment given by **Charles the Bald:** the **Holy Tunic** worn by the Virgin on the day of the Annunciation. The more sceptical of our readers should not smile too much: there is the same amount of mystery surrounding this tunic as there is the Holy Shroud of Turin.

What it is important to remember is that from then on Chartres was to be consecrated to the cult of the Virgin, and it is interesting to observe also that in the XIVth century the legend spread abroad of the **Virgo paritura** (Virgin about to give birth) who must have been worshipped in Gallo-Roman times. One can see the extremely smooth way in which widely different religious concepts fuse together in the sanctuary following a secret but definite logical process. The water cult develops into a cult of the Mother Goddess, and finally into the cult of the Virgin: fertility, maternity, purity, transcendence, and humanity come together in a most felicitous way. Bishop Gislebert's cathedral was constructed in 858 and all that remains of it is the Saint Lubin Crypt that is beneath the high altar. This cathedral was unfortunately to be destroyed by fire in 1020 but was reconstructed by Bishop Fulbert in 1024 along more ambitious lines than the previous one. The fame of Chartres had already spread well beyond our frontiers for the cathedral was reconstructed not only with the assistance of **Robert II,** King of France, but also with that of **Canut,** King of Denmark and England. The cathedral is therefore of an exceptional length in order to be able to welcome numerous pilgrims, and its proportions remained unique in French architecture of the Middle Ages. It is worth mentioning that at that time the principles of the buttress and the flying buttress were not sufficiently developed to be able to construct a vault suitable enough for a building of such a length. The weight of the roof therefore had to rest entirely on the walls. In 1134 the north belfry was completed; in 1145 the south belfry; and around 1170 the immense masterpiece which constitutes the **Royal Door.** Its three porches which form the principal entrance to the cathedral are not only representative of Romanesque statuary but also of the faith of the Middle Ages. Unfortunately Chartres seemed doomed to be consumed by fire and around 1190 a new fire broke out which destroyed a large part of the building, although the Royal Door stayed intact. A delightful anecdote emerged from this. The reader will remember that in the IXth century the tunic of the Virgin was donated to the cathedral. Now, when the fire broke out, some courageous priests attempted to save this precious relic but they could not leave the cathedral because the fire was burning so fiercely. They shut themselves up therefore in the Saint Lubin Crypt, and some days later, beneath the rubble, the Virgin's tunic was found intact and the priests were completely unscathed. News of this event spread far. Without any doubt God had intervened to save the sanc-

The nave, 53 ft. wide and 120 ft. high.

8

tuary, and despite the extent of the damage it was decided to return to the work of reconstruction with great enthusiasm and that boundless confidence and vitality which characterise the Middle Ages in France. Just as in heroic times when heroism itself was contagious, people vied with each other in generosity, the rich bringing much of their income (often indeed donating even their family silver), while the poor used their carts to carry stones weighing up to a ton over the eleven kilometres that separated Chartres from the quarries at Berchères. Chartres is above all a collective work, a work of faith, but also a work that brought together people who knew of the existence of greater things than the individual's isolated search for glory. 1260 was the date of the dedication of the cathedral. But let us not forget the history of the town. Its economic development under Philippe-Auguste was remarkable: different trades multiplied, particularly those so-called river trades at the head of which is flour milling. Chartres was going to hold the key to the granary of France. It was for this reason that it was frequently under siege, the most famous siege occuring during the 100 years' war. But let us not forget that this was Chartres, for a miracle came to save the town from disaster. Stones rained down from heaven, and this made Edward III retreat

and negotiate peace (the Treaty of Bretigny). After the sieges pilgrimages to Chartres became more frequent. Henri III walked there in 1583 "very weary with the soles of his feet covered in blisters on account of the long road", and this tradition as everyone knows has carried on down to our own day. The only thing that has changed is the road: "the highroad is our narrow gateway" wrote Charles Péguy.

Unfortunately, the care and concern that have always been shown the sanctuary led to some unnecessary additions being made to it in the XVIIIth century under the pretext of embellishment. Once the rood screen was destroyed it was considered advisable to create a new monumental decor which does not have the best effect. Earlier we were alluding to the effects of syncretism, but in the case of the sanctuary there is this inconsistency which can hardly be said to blend in well with the rest. However, let us not complain too much: the XIXth century spared Chartres, and that is something to be thankful for. And today, in spite of wars and fires (the last big fire was in 1836) we can admire a monument that is virtually intact, as long as the vicissitudes of history do not tax the patience of men beyond their endurance.

The cathedral

"The cathedral is a theological treatise. All these "Notre Dames" which stand in the principal towns of France are the ascension of the soul towards heaven. There is in the world no temple more intrinsically spiritual than Chartres cathedral".

(André MAUROIS).

This historical introduction seemed necessary to us in order to familiarise the reader and the visitor with the sufferings and the boundless joy of Chartres, for in the silent stones there are and there always will be, the memories of certain men who must

be brought to life again. Here we are now in front of the cathedral. A grave problem presents itself to the writer of a guide book. Must one write for the tourist who is hurrying to see just the bare essentials and has no time for detail, or for the enthusiast whose

The King David Window on the north wall of the transept.

curiosity has been aroused by something extraordinary ? In order not to displease everybody we have tried to write for the class that we hope is made up of the majority: honest and upright people. We would meanwhile strongly recommend that the enthusiast read the classical works of Fouillon and Emile Mâle who are certainly great experts in this field, but also a novel that is little read but which is extremely important — Huysman's **Cathedral** which is an exceptionally rich and precise introduction to medieval religious symbolism. André Maurois wrote that the cathedral is a theological treatise — it is not only an admirable means of expression, but it also contains profound truth. It is not just a question of looking at the cathedral but of reading it like a book and finding all the hidden meanings and secrets which are to be found in its lay-out. Everything **means something,** from the arrangement of the tympans to that of the pillars. The realms of sense and intellect overlap and complement each other perfectly. Thus the cathedral, far from being just the symbol of the world, is the very world it wishes to represent. There is nothing accidental in it and if emotions are to be well-founded they must involve understanding, or rather intellection, to use the medieval term.

The façade : the belfries
Romanesque purity and gothic richness ;
aesthetics and asymmetry

One can think of no more marvellous a contrast than that which exists between this Romanesque steeple, the finest perhaps in its striking simplicity which has ever been built, and the Gothic steeple flamboyantly adorned in every way. On one side is faith in all its original purity, and on the other a dazzling and triumphant indication of the end of the Middle Ages. This asymmetry in the façade gave the painter Carot an interesting problem in deplicting Chartres cathedral. He very aptly placed before the lower tower a small mound of earth surmounted by a tree which goes some way towards carrying through the lines of the steeple and accentuating it, and gives one the impression of its being almost identical to its proud counterpart. This is just one story concerning it. The south and the oldest belfry has been intact since the XIIth century, and the steeple is 105 metres high (this makes it the highest Romanesque steeple). The structure of the belfry is simple: an octagonal steeple arising from a square tower. Something to be noticed from the stylistic point of view is the extraordinary array of gables at the base of the steeple which accentuate its lines and give it a startling dynamic effect. What finer representation of medieval faith could one hope for than these simple lines without any superfluous decoration, as if the steeple were able to assure a passage without any intervening obstacles, from earth to heaven ? Let us point out to those who want technical details, which are most important in this connection, that on the one hand the steeple is hollow (there is no interior framework), and on the other each stone is like a scale, and this very intelligently stops the infiltration of water and also partly explains the steeple's perfect state of preservation which is also due to the excellence of the materials employed. The flamboyant steeple was built by Jean Texier, also know as Jean de Beauce, and was completed in 1513. It clearly abounds in flamboyant decoration which offers a most interesting and most enriching contrast with the neighbouring steeple. From pure mystical faith, from an immediate contact with the divine, we are transported

The mighty flying buttresses and piers made it possible to build huge stained glass windows.

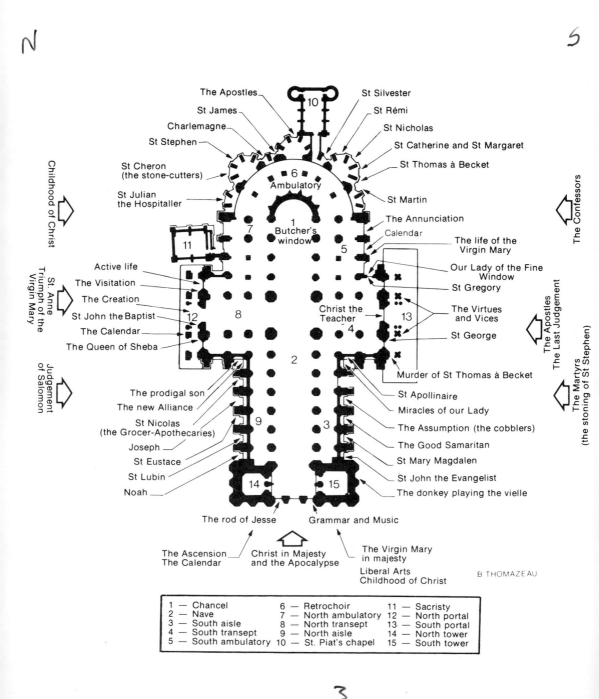

N

S

The Apostles
St James
Charlemagne
St Stephen
St Cheron
(the stone-cutters)
St Julian
the Hospitaller

St Silvester
St Rémi
St Nicholas
St Catherine and St Margaret
St Thomas à Becket

10

6
Ambulatory

St Martin

Childhood of Christ

The Confessors

1
Butcher's
window

7

11

5

The Annunciation
Calendar
The life of the
Virgin Mary

Active life
The Visitation
The Creation
St John the Baptist
The Calendar
The Queen of Sheba

St Anne
Triumph of the
Virgin Mary

12

8

Christ the
Teacher

4

13

Our Lady of the Fine
Window
St Gregory

The Virtues
and Vices

St George

The Apostles
The Last Judgement

Judgement
of Salomon

2

Murder of St Thomas à Becket

The Martyrs
(the stoning of St Stephen)

The prodigal son
The new Alliance
St Nicolas
(the Grocer-Apothecaries)
Joseph
St Eustace
St Lubin
Noah

9

3

St Apollinaire
Miracles of our Lady
The Assumption (the cobblers)
The Good Samaritan
St Mary Magdalen
St John the Evangelist
The donkey playing the vielle

14

15

The rod of Jesse

Grammar and Music

The Ascension
The Calendar

Christ in Majesty
and the Apocalypse

The Virgin Mary
in majesty
Liberal Arts
Childhood of Christ

B THOMAZEAU

1 — Chancel	6 — Retrochoir	11 — Sacristy
2 — Nave	7 — North ambulatory	12 — North portal
3 — South aisle	8 — North transept	13 — South portal
4 — South transept	9 — North aisle	14 — North tower
5 — South ambulatory	10 — St. Piat's chapel	15 — South tower

through the centuries to a religion where decoration was indispensable for it played the part of **mediator,** as if souls thenceforth were no longer capable of self-fulfilment and the gap between earth and heaven could be bridged with a single bound. Architecture became a spectacle, and hence it became spectacular. It must be pointed out, moreover, that Jean de Beauce in no way tried to esta-blish a harmory between his construction and the older steeple. The asymmetry which annoys us somewhat was then considered to be a sign of life, expressiveness etc... What must be remembered about this juxtaposition is that it is unique in its genre. Several centuries of religion are brought together before our eyes for those who know how to look.

The Royal Door. Christ Triumphant ; Sculpture and faith

It was sculptured between 1145 and 1150 and is of such fine quality that, alas, it defies description. It is consecrated to Christ the King Triumphant (look first of all at the tympan of the central arch). One of its more noticeable characteristics is the use of **statue columns** as splays which immediately give an impression of great humanity. It has not been possible to identify the characters portrayed here but it is generally agreed that they are from the Old Testament which would explain in an extremely simple way (and why not?) their symbolical function as pillars. The austerity and gravity of these striking figures, softened by a gentle smile which seems to appeal only to our deepest emotions, and which we shall become so familiar with that we shall always associate it with Chartres, is very characteristic of the finest Romanesque statuary. This Royal Door is surmounted by three windows (which we shall be returning to), and above these windows is the rose window with a radius of 7 metres (which is considerable), and which may be counted among the finest in Gothic art. This rose window is in turn surmounted by the **Kings' Gallery.** To return to the Royal Door, it is composed of three arches, each one relating to an episode in the life of Christ. On the right is the birth or Christ, and in the centre Christ in Glory.

The Right Arch (the childhood of Christ). He is seen in the tympan sitting on the knees of the Virgin being praised by two angels. Beneath the tympan in the two lintels are clear representations of scenes of the Annunciation, Visitation, Nativity and the Adoration of the Shepherds. In the scene with the shepherds is the delightful flautist who, bewildered by the news, holds his flute to his lips and opens his eyes wide with astonishment. Even in such an elevated piece of sculpture there is still room in the Middle Ages for such a charming anecdote, as if the artist were imparting life and striving to achieve realism in every detail. And this still enchants us even today. But of course we need to search carefully for these details and if we have the patience we shall be rewarded. The upper lintel, whose workmanship is poorer, relates the Presentation in the Temple. In the upper curves there are seven women representing the seven liberal arts, and below them are the seven sages of Antiquity (no need to draw attention to the importance and significance of the number seven throughout the Middle Ages), each one surmounted by a characteristic symbol. These sages are Priscien, Cicero, Pythagoras, Euclides, Ptolemy, Aristotle. Finally, it is important to underline the role of the interaction between the different architectural elements. "Real" history and spiritual history merge happily with one another as well as the masculine and feminine symbols that counterbalance each other in a Door that is dedicated to the glory of the Virgin and the glory of Christ. It must be remembered that medieval art always strives to achieve totality, and is thus completely different from our colourful modern art which seeks to break everything down and is non-finite.

The Left Arch (the Ascension of Christ). The Ascension of Christ is represented in the tympan. In the bottom lintel upturned angels come down from heaven and announce the news to the Apostles who raise their heads and look up. Thus in a very simple but most effective way a composition emerges which transcends the rigid architectural framework and opens the way for free "dialogue", if one may use the term, between the different parties concerned. In the curves above are

depicted the.signs of the Zodiac which alternate with seasonal scenes. It is of course not possible to mention here all these scenes but you must not miss Janus cutting up the Twelfth Cake, the admirable scorpion, the peasant slaughtering his pig. Simple daily tasks are also linked through the signs of the Zodiac to a higher level of meaning: that inherent in the tympan itself involving as it does the sanctification of human life through the Ascension of Christ who is delivering it from the anxiety of temporality and death.

The Central Arch (Christ in Glory). This is certainly the most important arch for it gives its name to the whole Door inspired by the Apocalypse of St. John. Christ in Majesty in the centre of the tympan illuminates the whole Door by his own very special physiognomy which ranges from gentle humanity to divine brilliance. The balance between the face (which paradoxically seems considerably more human than the slender, elongated faces on the columns which despite their smiles retain a certain grimness), and the soft and gentle folds of the robe, immediately underlines the spiritual radiation that shines forth from this statue of Christ. Note too that He is surrounded by symbols of the four Evangelists: the angel of St. Matthew, the lion of St. Mark, the eagle of St. John, and the bull of St. Luke. In the curves above can be seen angels and the old musicians of the Apocalypse. In the one and only lintel the Apostles converse without participating in any way in the scene above them. This is worth commenting on. In the arch devoted to the Ascension we saw that there was a relationship between the different parts. Here, on the other hand, Christ appears from now on in all the splendeur of his **transcendence,** that is to say that he is no longer participating fully in terrestrial life, and in a most extraordinary way the Apostles now are turned towards the spectator inviting him to share in the Good Tidings (Gospel derives originally from the Greek word for good news). Thus the Apostles become the interpreters of the word of Christ on earth. It was with consummate skill that medieval artists made use of architectural shapes and looked on them not as painful obstacles but as a means of moulding and reproducing ideas and symbols. The last thing to note about the Royal Door is the capitals surmounting the statue columns. They tell the story of Joachim and St. Anne (the parents of the Virgin), Mary, the childhood of Jesus according to the New Testament, but also according to the Apocrypha. You will easily identify the flight into Egypt, the massacre of the Innocents, the Last Supper, the kiss of Judas...

The interior architecture

"Tell me (because you are sensitive to architecture), have you not observed, on walking round this town, that among all the buildings in it some are dumb; others talk; and a very small number of others sing?".

Paul VALÉRY, *Eupalinos or the Architect.*

First some figures in order to have some precise idea about the dimensions of the buildings. It is 130 metres 20 cms. long and the nave is 16 metres 40 cms. wide (this is bigger than all the other Gothic cathedrals in the north of France), but remember that we have already established that the original Romanesque building, that was intended to be a place of pilgrimage, was particularly wide. The vault formed of interlinked ogives

The Pierre Mauclerc Window on the front of the south transept.

(Over the page)

The Royal Portal.

is 37 metres high. The most notable thing about the inside of the building besides the actual size is the height of the windows and the boldness of their architectural design is quite revolutionary from the point of view of style since they solve the main problem of how to bring light into the interior of the building. The galleries which look out over the nave in other buildings and thus take away some of the light have been replaced here by a gallery called the triforium. The windows are thus shown off to their greatest advantage. They are twin arches 7 metres high each being surmounted by a rose window. But let us not forget that aesthetic evolution in architecture often comes in the wake of technical evolution and it is above all the advent of the flying buttress outside the building which made it possible to build such large windows in the walls. The transept is particularly well designed and is flanked by side-aisles which is a rare feature. The choir is flanked by a double ambulatory: the disposition of the pillars and the vaults, all of which are different, together with the incomparable brilliance of the windows, are worth taking a close look at. You will notice meanwhile that the choir screen, that is of a later date since it was undertaken after the XVIth century (the decorative work went on until the XVIIIth century), is incongruous and does not conform with the spirit of the Middle Ages.

The windows
The miracle of Chartres : light

The windows are really remarkable as much for their quality as for their dimensions. There are 172 of them containing more than two thousand square metres of glass. The gentle glow which spreads from them all over the cathedral, the quite exceptional quality of their design, makes them unforgettable. The pieces of coloured glass have lost nothing of their original brilliance and you should notice the intelligent way in which the lead settings accentuate the design in their subtle and sober fashion. It is necessary to observe, and this is very important in the art of the stained glass window, that the lead settings play a decisive rôle by throwing the design into relief. One only has to observe stained-glass windows of later centuries where all too often the lead feebly traces the line of the actual design (and this only detracts from the aesthetic beauty of the window), to conceive an even greater admiration for these imperative and bold lines which are not there to provide outlines but to reinforce the impression of the whole. Let us never be prepared to reject simplicity because it is no longer in vogue.

This collection of stained-glass windows also bears witness to the spirit behind the foundation of the cathedral. We do not know the artists (apart from Clément de Chartres who was famous at the time and whose signature appears on a window at Rouen), but many of the windows are marked with images of the dedicatees who are generally guilds: apothecaries, cartwrights, carpenters etc. From this we have a most interesting and vivid document on the trades of the time. The window of the Assumption, among others, gives us a lesson on the art of the cobbler. Observe also the builders of cathedrals on their ladders and the sculptor in front of a roughly-hewn statue pausing for a few moments for a drink. You can see, therefore, the considerable importance of these windows both from an artistic and historic point of view. It should be pointed out that they do not all date from the same time. Those situated above the Royal Door were made at the same time as it was (around 1145). The others were made over a period between 1210 and 1235, and it would be around 1235 too that the rose windows of

The chevet seen from the south.

20

the transept and clerestories were glazed.

The three West windows. They survived the fire of 1194 and date therefore from the previous building. To the north there is a stem of Jess which is particularly remarkable because of the intensity of the blues. It represents the genealogy of Christ (the same theme was covered a short time before at Saint Denis). In the centre, 29 medallions recount episodes in the life of Jesus. Its dimensions are considerable: the window itself is about 11 metres high and is composed alternatively of round scenes with a blue background, and square scenes with a red background. It is surmounted by the Queen of Heaven.

The most celebrated of the windows of Chartres dates from the same time: **Our Lady of the Beautiful Window** (second window of the south ambulatory) which is striking because of the "pensive air" which Huysmans described so adequately. The exceptionally human and maternal quality of this face together with the discreet but most intense suggestion of the suffering that will inevitably come but which has already been accepted and even surmounted by quiet resignation; the extraordinary psychological power behind this face make this window one of the keys to our understanding of the spirit of Chartres that has its own special mysticism which belongs only to this sanctuary. The outstanding quality of the blue contrasting with the dark red background emphasises still more this idea of psychological intensity. The other windows, as we have already pointed out, are later. You should note especially the five representations in the high choir windows which are dedicated to Mary (Queen of Heaven, Annunciation, Visitation). In the barred

windows where there are representations of the Evangelists and scenes from the Apocalypse one cannot help but notice the faces of the Prophets and the startling whites of their eyes which gives them a most powerful and dramatic appearance. In the ambulatory you will observe the famous Charlemagne window which illustrates the Song of Roland. What must be remembered above all about these windows is the importance of the symbols behind them. Hence the Old Testament, the awaiting of the Messiah, figure on the nothern façade and are only lit up by the last rays of the summer sun. In the lancet-window of the choir, illuminated by the morning sun, can be seen the Coming of the Light of the World. The Last Judgement is oriented towards the setting sun and it clearly symbolises very simply the end of time, while the southern rose window displays Christ in Glory and is at its most brilliant when the light is at its brightest. It can be seen therefore that even the windows are arranged in a most subtle way so that the spectacle brings us as close as possible to the mystical truth. In order to facilitate an understanding of the windows, here are a few general guidelines:

Southern side aisle: St. John the Evangelist, St. Mary Magdalene, the Good Samaritan, Adam and Eve, the Window of the Assumption, the Window of the Miracles.

Northern side aisle: Noah and the Flood, St. Lubin, St. Eustace and his legend, the life of Joseph, the life of St. Nicolas, the Redemption.

Upper tier windows: Jean-Clément-du-Mez.

Nave: St. George, St. James, the Virgin of Wisdom.

Choir rose windows: Louis de France, Thibault, Compte de Chartres, Amavry.

Choir screen or a history of French statuary from the XVIth to the XVIIIth century : the spirit of Chartres in the face of Italian influence

The screen was built by the architect Jean de Beauce between 1514 and 1530 but its decoration was completed only in the XVIIIth century. Despite its great sculptural interest (above all a mixture of flamboyant Gothic and Italian influence, then numerous interesting items such as Jean Boudin's sculptures) it is somewhat out of place and on the whole is somewhat alien to the spirit of Chartres. The first four groups were sculptured by Jean Soulas between 1519 and 1525 (the history of St. Anne and St. Joachim, both parents of the Virgin, and the birth of the Virgin). An unknown artist did the eight following groups between 1525 and 1540 (Biblical episodes, Adoration of the Magi, the Presentation of Mary in the Temple). In 1542 François Marchand sculptured two particularly interesting groups: the Purification and the Massacre of the Innocents. In 1612 Thomas Boudin sculptured the Temptation of Jesus, the Canaanite, the Transfiguration. The following groups are the work of Jean de Dieu, Pierre Legros native of Chartres, Tuby le Jeune, and Simon Mazières. These forty scenes evolve over more than twenty metres and although of a completely different nature from the rest of sculpture at Chartres they are by no means less interesting: on the one hand by the variety of the décor and the abundance of decorative motifs such as the buttress and the stylobates; on the other, and this applies above all to the first groups, by the insight which they give us into the first infiltrations of Italian influence into France. It is of particular interest to note that certain of these groups are very close to the aesthetics of the contemporary Italian "sacro monte" where there coexist at one and the same time naive and yet somewhat ostentatious faith together with most effective drama. Let us spend a little more time on the first scenes such as the Adoration of the Magi which is somewhat lacking in spiritual elevation. We should not be completely indifferent, however, to the benign serenity and the fine composition which conjure up immediately for us Italian painting. The choir which is even later is particularly notable for its richly embellished high altar designed by Charles-Antoine Bridan and built between 1767 and 1773, and which dazzles quite unashamedly. There is Italian influence here but perhaps not in its better aspects.

Unfortunately for Western art the influence of Bologna is still great... we should not feel too strongly about the Assumption of the Virgin in a bank of clouds.

The Crypt

It is composed of two parallel galleries joined by an ambulatory off which are three chapels. It all dates from the beginning of the eleventh century and corresponds with the foundation of Saint-Fulbert's cathedral. We had the opportunity to bring up this matter in the historical introduction. You can see the Saint Forts' well whose waters were considered to be miraculous in the Middle Ages as revealed by various depictions of miracles in the sanctuary. The well was filled up in the twelfth century by the people of Chartres. Just next door is the chapel of Our Lady beneath the Ground which used to contain the famous **Virgo paritura** burned by the revolutionaries, but the most important thing which one cannot fail to notice in the crypt is the extraordinary effect produced by the remains of the rood screen. This rood screen was put up under Saint Louis: it was made up of seven vaulted arches and was destroyed in 1763 and the mutilated statues were buried afterwards. Some were rediscovered beneath the flagged floor of the choir in 1849. These statues are now exhibited in the Saint Piat chapel and constitute the most beautiful example of Chartres fine art of the thirteenth century. The Nativity in particular, is, and always will be, famous. The quality of the composition, the verisimilitude of gesture, and in particular the gesture of tender solicitude as the Virgin touches her child, skilfully counterbalanced by her arm which remains resting on His head subtly conveying an exchange of feelings, make this a model of statuary. The exhaustion of the Magi does not detract from the quality of the finished work. It is quite remarkable to see how the artist has placed two scenes side by side in order to create a single one, thus bringing together under one guise the before and the after, the cause and the consequence. Laying aside its aesthetic value, we cannot remain indifferent to its high intellectual and even philosophical appeal. In fact, in a most extraordinary way, we find ourselves invited to witness an example of extra-temporal causality. The work is suspended in time, removed from all other contingencies. From history as an anecdote (and it is delightful to note what appears to be a certain tenderness in the artist himself on account of the anecdotal quality of the subject) we pass to History with a capital H, even from a medieval viewpoint. We should not put an end to our visit before having given just consideration to the Good Tidings to the Shepherds and the Presentation in the Temple, or before having noticed the bas-relief of animal figures and hunting scenes, and finally before having looked at the different keystones of

Christ, the four Evangelists, the Virgin and Angels, and the Annunciation. It may be mutilated and incomplete, but we should doubtless rejoice that it has not been entirely removed from our admiration. This rood screen is one of the most interesting items in Chartres cathedral. It was said by Jean-Paul Benoît, without exaggeration, that the genius of Chartres could all be found in it. Inside the cathedral there are still certain items which require special mention: **Our Lady of the Pillar, the veil of the Virgin, the Treasure, the Organ.**

We have been able to date the statue known as Our Lady of the Pillar from around 1500 (perhaps 1507). It is carved in pear wood and the original colours of the paint-work can still be seen. It was in former times called **The Black Virgin,** and by a happy chance it escaped savage destruction at the hands of the revolutionaries. It is positioned on a column of the old rood screen, hence its name, Our Lady of the Pillar.

The Treasure of the cathedral may be visited in the Saint Piat chapel (an interesting construction of the fourteenth century); the stained glass windows are mostly contemporary; the window representing the Virgin and Child with the donor kneeling before them dates from the XVIth century.

The most famous object of this Treasure is of course Our Lady's Veil, a gift from Charles the Bald, of which we have already spoken, and which is the subject of the dedication of the cathedral. It is interesting to know that, according to tradition, this was not a veil but a shirt. This was only discovered in 1712 after the opening of the first shrine, hence the medallion in the shape of a shirt worn by Chartres pilgrims. There are various pieces of gold to be seen in the Treasure: a chalice offered by Henry III, two gold hearts presented as votive offerings by Louis XVIth and Madame Elisabeth, a large XIIIth century casket resembling a triptych and decorated with Limoges enamel, a XVIth century ivory and gold cross, a XIIIth century bishop's crook, and a XIVth century incense-boat. You will notice to one side a certain number of votive offerings consisting movingly of belts sent by Iroquois Indians in the XVIIIth century. It can be seen that the influence of Chartres hardly knew any limits. The eagle lectern with its imposing proportions dates from 1726. The **organ** was finished in 1542 and stands on a balcony which dates from the XIVth century.

Let us now return to the outside of the cathedral. A word first of all about the very important **flying buttresses** for we have seen that they allowed the windows to be put in with their extraordinary height and the construction of a nave that is particularly wide. They are double flying buttresses, joined together by arcades and small columns. To complete this picture, supplementary flying buttresses were installed in the XIVth century (built onto the top). The flying buttresses rest on simple buttresses whose powerful austerity has the mark of the Romanesque spirit.

The north façade door

First a porch, added in the XIIIth century between 1224 and 1230 under the reign of Philippe-Auguste, shelters these three transept doors. It is made up of three cradle-vaults resting on finely-decorated columns. Many statues are missing (yet more victims of the Revolution) but among those that remain are the Kings and Queens of Juda, the Prophets, Saint Potentien and his episcopal mitre, Saint Modeste and Bethsheba. The three archways contain curves which are decorated. On the right the signs of the Zodiac are parallel to the months of the year. Certain details are charming: Winter is warming his feet; Summer is laden with foliage. In the central archway is represented the Creation of the World which concludes with illustrations of human work: Adam digs

Top: The south side of the cathedral and St. Piat's Chapel, built between 1323 and 1350.

Bottom: General view of the cathedral above the rooftops of the town.

while Eve spins, and God blesses their labours. It would appear that human work is considered to be a form of redemption from original sin and it is for this reason that it takes its place in the story of the Creation. The whole door is admirable and merits special attention. On the left, in the exterior curves may be seen illustrations of an active and a contemplative life. The fourteen Beatitudes are symbolised by feminine figures. The illustrations are all extremely varied and depict different trades (wool, linen and hemp).

The Central Door which dates from the very beginning of the XIIIth century is consecrated to the Glorious Virgin. One can see in the tympan and in the lintel the death of Mary (more frequently referred to as the **Dormition,** or "sleeping", for, according to Christian tradition, Mary is spared death. This theological detail is not out of place here for this is the reason why there are no tombs inside Chartres cathedral, as opposed to numerous other similar places. The image of death is in fact bannished from the cult of the Virgin). At the side, still in the lintel, is the Assumption and in the tympan is a representation of the Virgin's coronation. Beneath a canopy Christ crowns His Mother. They are flanked by two angels. On the splays are saints and prophets predicting the advent of Mary, Melchisadech, Abraham (about to sacrifice Isaac), Moses and the bronze serpent, Aaron or Samuel (?), David, Isaias represented above the sleeping Jesse, Jeremiah, Simeon, St. John the Baptist (the most remarkable of all the statues), Saint Peter (observe the parallel between Saint Peter and Melchisadech : the New and Old Law). On the pier, a pensive St. Anne carries the child Mary. Observe also the symbolical presence of the man at the base of Jeremiah's statue on the one hand, and at the base of Simeon's on the other. Finally, in the curves the line of David is represented symbolically by the branches of a tree of Jesse, a frequent adornment as we have already pointed out.

The Right Door. This was apparently decorated arpund 1220. It is consecrated to characters in the Old Testament and illustrates the idea of human wisdom. On the splays are Balaam on his she-ass, Solomon and the Queen of Sheba. Notice the graceful movement of the Queen turning towards Solomon, and the charming effigy of the black servant beneath the Queen. At the base is the fool Marcoulf. Then come Jesus Ben Sira, author of the Ecclesiastes, Judith with her feet on her dog, Joseph, son of Jacob — at the base is the temptation of Potiphar. On the lintel you will notice the famous scene of Solomon's judgement and on the tympan the sufferings of Job covered with ulcers by Satan to make him renounce his faith. In the curves are told the stories of Samson, Gideon, Esther, Judith and Tobias. Once more there is a symbolical reason behind the choice of these characters, for they are characters from the Old Testament that foreshadow the Virgin and Christ. Those that can truly understand this can see the close symbolic parallels between this door and the central door.

The Left Door. Once again this is dedicated to the Virgin and to the child Jesus. On the splays are Isaiah, Gabriel (whose head was unfortunately lost and was replaced in 1959), Daniel, Saint Elisabeth, the Virgin. One can hardly fail to react to the movement which brings this piece of statuary to life. The characters turn towards each other to converse, and they are surrounded by a feeling of liberty and serenity. On the tympan are represented the birth of Christ, the Apparition of the Angels to the Shepherds, the Adoration and the dream of the Magi. On the curves above are statues that counterbalance each other representing Virtue and Vice, and the Wise Virgins and the Foolish Virgins.

The Madonna and Child in Glory at the top of the great west window.

The south façade

Let us start once more by the porch that was built after the doors themselves. The porch of the southern end of the transept dates probably from 1224. Unlike the north porch it does not have any statues on the splays. The main pillars are decorated with twenty four medallions. On the front of two of these pillars are the old musicians of the Apocalypse. On the others are the Virtues and Vices. The Virtues are sitting on thrones and carry their own coats of arms. They stand out above everything else for they are timeless. It is interesting to see in fact that the artist has voluntarily avoided an anecdotal approach in order to retain this intellectual quality. On the other hand the Vices are right in the forefront of the action. One can judge the effectiveness of this juxtaposition for the vices are the incarnation of all that is contingent and temporal (and this presupposes the necessity of redemption in order to pass from one state of being to another), while the Virtues are simply an incarnation of all that is pure. As for the scenes representing the Vices, they are full of spontaneity, freshness and vivacity: Despair, piercing himself with his own sword; Avarice, diving into his chest; Pride, thrown from his horse; Callousness, beating his benefactor; Cowardice, running away from a rabbit and dropping his weapon; Inconstancy depicted as a monk throwing away his cowl, if not to the winds then certainly in front of the monastery door; Discord is a domestic scene showing a broken pitcher and an abandoned spindle. We have already noted frequently in the stained glass windows and also in the statuary the importance of the theme of work and the "blessing" which accompanies it, either in the literal sense (remember God blessing the works of Adam and Eve) or the moral sense as in this scene. It is worthwhile pointing out that apart from the primary task of spiritual edification, the artists, always sensitive to the everyday world around them, never omitted to underline the down-to-earth side of faith. You will notice too, on the left splays, the Confessors St. Lumer, St. Leon, St. Ambrose, St. Nicolas.

The south façade door : (Central door)

It is dedicated to the Last Judgement and dates from the years 1210 to 1215. On the pier, there is the key to the meaning of the whole door for Christ is there teaching (He is teaching the Apostles who figure on the splays) and he is carrying the Bible and giving blessing with His right hand. One is affected by the majestic simplicity of this statue, this mixture of somewhat harsh convention and softness, created by a skilful interplay of straight and oblique lines. There is no need to dwell on the importance of this figure in the centre of this doorway. The proximity of the scenes of the Resurrection and the Last Judgement underline unequivocally the importance of the word of Christ for whomsoever wants salvation. The decoration is not there simply for decorative purposes. On the splays, then, are the Apostles with their respective attributes: St. Matthew, St. Philip, St. Thomas, St. Andrew, St. Peter, St. Paul, St. John, St. James the Greater, St. James the Less, and St. Bartholomew. Their feet are crushing the heads of their tyrants or their executors. In the lintel, the Archangel St. Michael separates the Chosen and the Damned. The procession of the Chosen in which all social ranks are represented, moves from right to left and on the right, the Damned are thrown into the jaws of Hell. Again in this instance, all the social ranks are represented (note here and there the presence of a king and a bishop). A king exchanges his own crown for that of one of the Chosen. Earthly vanity is an omnipresent theme in medieval statuary.

Salomon

(Over the page)
The sumptuous beauty of the transept.

30

In the tympan, Christ, bare to the waist, reveals his wounds, flanked by Mary and St. John. All around are angels carrying the instruments of the Passion. In the curves of the arch are the nine choirs of angels.

The left door or the Martyrs' door

It was made between 1215 and 1220. The statues on the splays represent St. Theodore, St. Stephen with St. Sens close by, St. Clement and St. Lawrence, St. Piat, St. Denis, St. Vincent and St. George. Two statues were added a little later, probably towards 1230, and one in the guise of knights (the one opposite St. George probably represents Roland). Without any doubt they merit being called perfect. The lintel, the tympan and the bottom row of the curves tell of the stoning of St. Stephen by the Jews. He is raising his eyes towards Christ who figures on the tympan between two kneeling angels, wearing the royal crown and carrying the Martyr's palm. In the upper curves are Martyrs and Holy Innocents collecting the blood of the lamb. Here again we should note the striking unity of inspiration, for no door can be viewed independently from the next. It is certain that the glorification of the Martyrs in this instance must complement the double allegory of the central door: the teaching of Christ and the Last Judgement, the exact rôle of the Martyrs being to guarantee the necessary link between Christ's word and St. Michael choosing souls.

The right door or the Confessors' door

This is the final panel of our triptych. It dates from 1220 to 1225 and is dedicated to the Confessors, that is to say to all those who have fought for the faith. It therefore completes symbolically the so-called Martyrs' Door. Virtue through example is now followed by Virtue through the spoken word. On the splays are St. Laumer, St. Leon wearing the pontifical tiara, St. Ambrose, St. Nicolas, St. Martin of Tours, St. Jerome reading the biblical text written on parchment that is unrolled to the base of the pillar which the members of the synagogue are trying to decipher with their eyes blindfolded, and finally St. Gregory and St. Avit. In the same way as in the previous door, the first and last of these statues are later additions, these being St. Laumer and St. Avit (two local saints) which are of quite remarkable workmanship that stands out against the roughness of the other statues. On the lintel and on the tympan are stories of the life of St. Martin (St. Martin asleep next to his valet, St. Martin sharing his cloak), and of St. Nicolas (St. Nicolas giving his purse to a poor man, the curing of pilgrims by the miraculous oil flowing from St. Nicholas' tomb). In the curves are certain saints and also the legend of St. Giles. Forty eight episodes from the lives of the saints are carved on the angular pillars of the porch. Among them let us point out on the Confessors' pillar first of all, the baptism of Clovis by St. Remy, St. Antony visited by the Devil; and on the Martyrs' pillar, St. Eustace on the fiery bull, St. Lawrence on the rack, St. Blaise flayed, the beheading of St. John the Baptist, St. Vincent protected by wild animals, and the decapitation of Thomas Becket in Canterbury cathedral. Their meaning completes the double message of the doors: that of the word of Christ and that of the Martyrs of the Faith, thus reinforcing the idea of unity which impresses one throughout the visit to the cathedral.

The Aaron Window in the north wall of the transept.

The episcopal palace and its gardens

The **façade** dates from the reign of Louis XIII. The mixture of pink brick and white chiselled stones gives the best of effects. The palace was built on the orders of Bishop Léonor d'Estampes de Valençay. Two bishops restored it in the XVIIIth century: Monsignor de Godet de Marais and Monsignor de Rosset de Fleury (the latter in particular is noteworthy for having built the entrance pavilion which dates from 1748). A visit to the interior of the palace is particularlyworthwhile. You will note in the Hall of Honour the double **flight of stairs of wrought iron** designed by Germain; the **Italian Room** encircled by a gallery, and designed by the architect Godot. The rosescarved into the walls are the arms of Monsignor de Fleury. The **chapel,** built by Rousset, is remarkable on account of the elegance of its proportions and constitutes a most interesting example of French religious architecture of the XVIIIth century. The altar also dates from the XVIIIth century and is surmounted by a Virgin which is a mere cast of a statue of the Assumption by Bridan. You will notice the quite exceptional group of the twelve Apostles, worked in enamel by Leonard Limousin for François I. Apart from their rare aesthetic quality, they are exceptional because of their size. Coloured marble marquetry-work on the floor reminds one once again of the Fleury roses. The reception rooms contain art collections. First there are medieval objets d'art: chased enamel work (pixis, crook, processional cross, reliquary), a bronze measure dated 1283, an embroidered triptych dating from the XVth century, and important illuminated manuscripts; sculptures; a XIIth century Christ the King, a very remarkable XVth century Virgin with Child, and a XIIIth century St. John the Evangelist. But most important of all are the impressive collections of paintings where numerous schools are represented. Let us point out a Virgin of the Fra Angelico school, Zurbarán's Saint Lucy of great psychological intensity, Holbein's Erasmus, Mignard's portrait of Molière, Turenne by Philippe de Champaigne, Fontenelle by Largillière, the child Duke of Saint-Simon by Rigaud, many Fragonards (and many Fragonard and Coypel drawings). You should note also the collections of tapestries decorating the XVIIIth century drawing room: Moses (Brussels, XVIth century), Maximilian hunting (Gobelins) and the Love Affaire of the Gods, a series of tapestries in the style of several of Boucher's works. Other rooms are full of contemporary paintings, arms, folklore, folk art, and items from Antiquity and the Far East. Your visit should end in the pleasant gardens.

PHOTOGRAPHIC CREDITS

Hervé Champollion: 9, 14, 16, 17 and back cover.
Nicolas Fédiaevsky: 7, 28, 29.
Jean-Paul Gisserot: 2, 11, 19, 22 and front cover.
Mgr Roger Michon: 4, 5, 24, 26, 31.

Front cover: View of the cathedral high above the town.

Back cover: The west front seen from the close with the two towers 341 ft. and 374 ft. high.

Translated by paul williams

© 1986 - SECALIB — I.S.B.N. 2.86797.044.X — Dépôt légal : 2e trimestre 1986 — 044.01.09.06.86
Imprimerie Raynard, La Guerche-de-Bretagne - Photogravure couleurs Ouest-France.